HEAVEN IN HELL

ESPRIT MASQUE

Dedicated to All...

Contents

Contents

Contents

Foreword

she had a voice,
a voice which was shut
a voice which was blunt ;
a voice which was louder than
a lion's roar.

Preface

unlimited stories; incomplete
unheard and denied by the society
'cause darling wasn't it all a taboo
yet when one inks those
stories gives voice to those stories
they are the bad ones .
a flaw to the so-called perfect society.

Acknowledgements

ESPRIT MASQUE,

Would like to thank everyones involvment in the book and appreciate the confidence their friends had in them . Specifically naming them are currently not possible yet they very well know who they are and how much they have supported the poet in this journey of ups and downs . Some since the beginning of the journey and some recently yet equally meaningful and gracious .

Thank you all for the hope you held in me .

Prologue

Just like how
the great poetess
who wrote
about death; wasn't dead
just 'cause she writes about
love she doesn't become
a lover.

Chapter1

I should've listened
I should've been aware
I should've distanced; but
I didn't. No matter how much
I've been put down
I rise and fall. But yet
I thought this would last
This would be my happiness But No
I have changed, a lot actually I have a smile that I'm pretty sure would never fade.

Chapter2

I close my eyes, I
See you, I open my eyes
I miss you. All where I've been
I see you, close; but every
The moment I come close you
Seem to disintegrate.
Our love was pure as crystal
But as always they took us
Away As the value of society
Meant more than a person's
Heart. I'll wait all my life Cause
You were a pain so deep
That you left a scar in me so
Long.

Chapter3

"I'll wait ,like
Juliette waited for her romeo
Rapunzel for her Ugine
Anna for her cristoff ,
But could you ,
Promise Me;
That you'd come , when
This wait would end ?
No .
Its like cinderella once said
"Waiting for you is like
Waiting for it to rain in this
Drought;useless and disappointing ""

Chapter4

I'm from the west
Where they consider
Pride over character
She's from the East
Where they consider
Beauty over confidence
He's from the North
Where they consider
Wealth over self esteem.
But ; your from the worst ,
Where you consider the number of friends or tweets define a
Human soul .But hey; I was
In love now wasn't I
Just tell me ;
"How many likes is my life worth "

Chapter5

I looked back ,
Our eyes met .

Chapter6

Since childhood;
She was one
Who loved shiny
Things Maybe that's
Why she fell In love with your
Glowing Face that night .
She had a dark soul
Maybe that's why You
Both looked like the night
Stars ;
Completely different,yet so much in love.

Chapter7

Having a penetrated
Heart, I didn't
Know, where I belonged
Each time you came
Across my heart
Skipped a beat.
I never knew, if
It was a crush or love
All I knew is that a day
Without seeing you felt like
Years.A minute without your
Laughter made me go deaf.
I never knew if you'd
Recognize me or not
But all I know is; that your
The only one that crosses my mind .

Chapter8

There was this storm
Late at night, I looked
All around, but you
We're not there; you
Said you'd be there but
You werent. You left,
For her; why, was I not enough
Did I not satisfy you...
NOW; Are you there for
Her? What did she do that I didn't
Was it so wrong to
love you.
Trust you .
But hey , I'm fine knowing
Your happy .I'll just keep
Searching for myself in
The pieces you shattered me to .

Chapter9

I was one with
Lots of expectations;
I fancied our life
To be as sweet as candy
And bitter as salt.
Yeah,
I expected the roses
Yeah ,
I expected the hugs
I expected the hugs ;
But I never expected you
To leave . Was it so wrong to
Love you ,Expect the same back .
You broke me apart and those
Pieces are lost . Lastly ,
I expect to see you above my coffin .

Chapter10

You said you
Don't care, but your
Eyes speak
A better truth.
You said you
Don't love but
Your tears spelled
His name.
You say you don't
Change but you
Die each day with
The thought of him.
You try, but no his
Name got engraved
In your heart. His
Ignorance made you
Swell but yet you chant
His name, Why.
I don't know what this
Is, is this an infatuation
Or unrequited love .

Chapter11

We started with a "hey"
And began with an
"I love you ".From staring
At you from a corner to
Having you close by; hoping
They don't misunderstand
To inviting them over.
From being scared to
Hold hands.
To wearing your last name.
My first love became my last.

Chapter12

She wanted to yell
It out but didn't;
She wanted to know but couldn't.
Every minute you spend
With another She would
Completely fall apart,
But yet smile a support towards
You .
She was busy at the moment
But would make time for you .
You fight , you scold,but
She smiles and says
He fights 'cause he knows
He scolds 'cause he cares .
But all that
Doesn't bother you
'Cause apparently your the
One with an open heart and she's
The one who's shallow.

Chapter13

• 13 •

Why do you love me?
My voice is never heard
My opinions were never bothered
I was never loved
I was never wanted
The ones who are close to
me left me.
Said she with gloom on her face.
He smiled and said; I
Can hear your voice. I
Care about your opinions
You'll always be loved by me.
You said you were never wanted
The only reason something is
Useless is when it's not understood.
They may have given
You to this universe,
But I understand you.

Chapter14

Why did you kill
Me with your words ?
Why did those Dovey words
Kill me .

Chapter15

When I was 5
My parents taught me
Not to get addicted to
Sweets.
When I turned 10
They told me not to
Talk to strangers.
When I was 15
They told me the danger
Behind drugs.
They taught me not to get
addicted to sweets
as they could give me
Sugar rush.
They taught me not to
Talk to strangers as
They were not all
Trustable.
Not to go into drugs
As they could harm me.
They taught me how to
Stay away from many things.
But; they never taught me not
To fall in love. They never warned
Me; about the toxin of obsession

I was obsessed, obsessed with all
Your filthy lies .

Chapter16

"Tell me who you are "
Something she has
Never heard.
"Your eyes speak your
Past ;
They're filled with fury
Hate
Betrayal
But
In a corner I spot love .
I see the love you have ."

Chapter17

When I was about 2
My parents got divorced
Since then it was just
Me and my brother .Three
Days at mom's and 3 days
At dad's,Our lives revolved till
I was 5 thus went on.
Then my brother started
Working ,he brought back my
Laughs. And now he's gone
Far -far gone .
Why you leave me here .
What could I do without you.
I remember one old day
I was crying at night and
My brother confronted me .
I asked him 'how he wasn't upset'
and
He replied "its not that I'm
Not upset ,it's that in every
Pain I hide mine with a smile ."
And now
I hide mine with the same smile
Said she at her brothers
Funeral .

Chapter18

I've always wanted to say
Yet I shut my mouth, not
Because I don't love ;
but cause I do .
and deep down I fear if
this love would
end us
once and for all

Chapter19

Let's build
our own love story chico
Let's be us, the real us
The flaws the fights the tears
Not a fairytale
But a tale; for ourselves to
Look back to

Chapter20

Apparently Parallel lines
Don't meet.
Yet we did stand side by side.
Throughout life,
Years and years went by
Yet we never changed.

Chapter21

Maybe loosing
Someone who meant
everything
To her:
Made her fearless

Chapter22

Never realized how your
"Oh, your leaving?"
Could make this heart flutter.

Chapter23

"I don't wanna be perfect
He wanted to make mistakes
She wanted to be flawfull
She wanted to be free
He wanted to be consoled
You wanted to be felt
Said everyone to themselves
-our generation really is under a mask
A mask of truth.

Chapter24

I always loved your smile,
but as time passed by
it started to fade, maybenot cause of me nor you but
I think you should go now
as I said I love your smile;
but. now for its existence we
should let go.
Just always; remember someone somewhere is smiling
knowing your happy.

Chapter25

The thought of loosing you made me quiver,
I would die the second I loose you.

Chapter26

Stuck between,
"I never want to feel
That type of pain again"
And
I want to feel that type of
Love again
From the same person over and over again.

Chapter27

It's amazing, what
A little bit of air
in our blood can
Do to our heart .

Chapter28

Is it love if it hurts?

Wasn't love supposed to be perfect?

Was it a misunderstanding?

If it was real?

Weren't we communicating ?

Were you there like said?

Or were you running?

Was I there like I said?

Or was I the one running ?

Chapter29

What were we?
How did 2 people
Who laughed together
Run?
How did life take such
A turn?
Why was my then butterflies
Now fear?
Why was my once happiness
My reason for anxiety?
Why were we separated by
Just a mere understanding?
Since when did we let other people come between us ?
When were we separated?

Chapter30

Going through our
Story, knowing it will
Hurt
Reading through the
Messages or stupidity
And forgiveness.
Enduring the memories
Of our once happy
Laughter and tears.
Remembering everyday
Like it happened yesterday.
Why does it still hurt?
Why does it hurt if it was nothing?
Why does it kill ,little by little .
Never had I thought I could give you up.

Chapter31

She focused all her
Attention towards things
Of no matter
Cause she knew
If she started to think
It would sum up to him.

Chapter32

• 33 •

How did the
Does an Angel turn into a devil?
After loosing everything
She lived for.

Chapter33

It is in the 'maybes'
she found hope.
It was in the 'what if's
she found fear
And it was in the future
she held on to.

Chapter34

Why is everyone bothered
About having a perfect
Happy ending?
How is the end of something
Somebodies happiness?
Let's not be like that,
Let's search for a
Beautifully imperfect flawfull
Yet Happy beginning.

Chapter35

Time after time
Every fantasy has to end.

Chapter36

Was that strength?
Being able to live through;
With no life.

Chapter37

It angered her,
Even when she was alone .
Created chaos in her mind
She wanted to scream ;
She wanted to shout,
But didn't: cause
She couldn't.
So she had to master herself
And in the journey of trying
She ruptured ,crippled
And dejected.
But no being took for granted
Was nothing new to her.

Chapter38

Flowing through her
Heart was her love for him
Yet she held the courage to
Say NO.

Chapter 39

He was the day.
She was night;
He was light,
she was rain
He was fire
She was water.
completely different; yet so much in love.

Chapter40

Too little to remember
Too much to forget

Chapter41

Smiling through
What feels like hell was
Always simple for him
That's how he lived life.

Chapter42

• 43 •

"One more strike
And you would turn ice " said her friends
You could see this ice walk on fire
And not melt.

Chapter43

Maybe : just maybe

Letting go was the

Best decision.

Chapter44

And sometimes they walk away
Not cause their out of love :
But cause, they know their
Love ;could ruin everything.

Chapter45

She showed the world

her dark side

so as to prevent her

heart from

Being broken:

But many a-times did she wish

She could be her self .

Chapter46

And maybe he wanted to scream

Maybe he wanted to cry

Maybe he wanted to burst

But held it all in for the time being

Chapter47

"Chemistry Says ;
Old bonds break when new ones are
formed "
Yet no bond could ever break ours.
"Euclid said;
Lines that go side by side end when
together"
Yet we could be side by side and together
with no fear.
"Shakespeare said;
Love was pain and beauty "
Yet ours was simply the best thing I've ever
had
Maybe cause neither of us went by the
rules,
Maybe cause neither of us liked the
ordinary
Maybe, our risks was what made us,us.
And maybe that's why we were unique.

Chapter48

Face your fears
You fear heights :
Skydive
You fear water :
Scuba dive
You fear socializing:
Party hard
Cause doing what you fear :
Changes your perspective on
Everything.

Chapter49

My heart found you
Mine found yours
Everything was sudden
We were in love
A type of love thot
Was unbreakable, unbearable
And uncontrollable
But then it was all over, again
All in a sudden but yet it's hard to forget the memories of
yours as I loved you
More than my very soul: this
Love is Painful cause it's been
long live been trying to
Move on but as my heart beats
It aches for you too.

Chapter50

Permanence
And maybe we were like parallel
Lines, always by each other.
Yet never meet.
Ever
Yeah, maybe we are
Parallel lines but the change of
Story is this time we will meet
And never drift apart.

Chapter51

• 52 •

The feeling you get
When the person who
Used to care for you so much
One day isn't bothered about you

Chapter52

Romeo must have been so
Worried loving Juliette;
Afraid he might loose her ...
Why's he drink the poison ?
Perhaps he knew , to love
Someone is to give them ;
Everything

Chapter53

Shut stuck caged
Yet she had hope.Hope
For herself, hope that
Someone would be there
In the dark hallow.But every time
She turned; herself puffed
With hope ;
The place was empty dark
And shallow.

Chapter54

Dreams were shattered ;
By painting Someone else's dream
Into reality.

Chapter55

In the fast world
Everything fades; Love,
Hate, sadness, anger
Family, friends, people
But; the words of a poet
Would never.
As his words; all have
A tremendous meaning
And a past which only
His listeners could feel .

Chapter56

She got tempered ; fast
Causing people to doubt
Once she was asked
Why, and the lady behind
Her answered 'cause she's
Under her own control '

Chapter57

We forget what the mind tells
Us cause we're more focused on
What our heart feels

Chapter58

The day we talked was magical;
A feeling not all understand.
You were different; the way we
Talk, disturb, laugh, smile, and
Fought was all my favorite
Your advice sure made me your
But also take to heart. Your
Cupidly smile and creaky hair
Is just so how perfect you are.
The way you defend, the way
You correct, the way you
Advice just made me fall.
You were like an oyster
So hard-cored yet so pleasent
Your shine was soo bright
That I went blind and
Walked right into your heart.

Chapter59

Our friendship
Our foolishness, our laughs.
Turn right you see them
Kissing; turn left you see
Them hugging. In a world
Where holding hands and
Locking lips is considered
Love all I ask for you
Is to be happy knowing your
Mine...

Chapter60

A feeling of being alone
Something that never left
My side. My best friend was
Loneliness. My words were
My comfort. But now
I'm done, done falling
Apart. So, I say 'I am a
20 year old; and these
Are my final wordings

Chapter61

"The moon and the
Sun was a perfect
Couple. One rise the other
Sets." "The earth and trees;
So unique, how about like
Them" she said once.
Are you sure said her lawyer
As she signed the divorse papers

Chapter62

• 63 •

We loved ;

Purely dearly

But things weren't that simple

Chapter63

Oh, sweet Betrayal!
Why are you always by
My side, why'd you love
Me so much? That you kept bestowing your so-called
Blessing on to me.
Oh, sweet Betrayal,
Why weren't you as sweet
As they say?
Oh , sweet Betrayal
Leave me be.
Oh, sweet Betrayal let's
Make a deal; you choose
Turn the page or shut the book .

Chapter 64

I fell In love with you
The first time I saw
You .you weren't just the
Most amazing guy I ever met .And somehow you chose me .
But how I loved you then;
It's nothing compared to how
I love you now .
Now I love you with
Everything inside of me .
But I think you should go now ;
I love you so much , I want you
To be happy , even if that happiness
No longer includes me .

Chapter65

It's always been you
It's always gonna be you ,
I can't accept any replacements.

Chapter66

I always felt , easy
To discuss all my
Life with you .
Remember that
Day when they
Told me you
Were not ; I challenged
Them ; but ...
It hurts actually,
Knowing I always
Talked about the
Devil to a devil.

Chapter67

He had to leave
And I couldn't stop
Him.I wanted to but ...
We were not long-term;
A balance of loyalty
And trust. Maybe things
Would work out or
Maybe things won't.
Either way ; I knew
" a part of me would
Always belong to him"

Chapter68

She had tears in her eyes
Thats when he understood
"All that glitters isn't gold"

Chapter69

Did the sun ever really leave the moon ?

Chapter70

They still look
At those times with joy
In their faces
Knowing it would never return .
Cause now , it was too late
A Lil too late
Nothing could be done
Except for them to hold on to
Themselves
And accept life
And maybe that's
What God has written for them
Ultimate amount of memories
Laughter and joy to haunt us for eternity .
Not every story has an ending
Some just go on within themselves .

Chapter71

She could see her future in his eyes

Epilogue

To be continued
cause life just goes on and on